Our Dead Behind Us

EX LIBRIS

W·W·NORTON & COMPANY·NEW YORK·LONDON

Our Dead Behind Us

POEMS BY Audre Lorde

Some of these poems have appeared in:
The Black Scholar
Ikon
Parnassus: Poetry in Review
Woman Poet: The East
Azalea
Conditions
Difference (Australia)
Sage: A Scholarly Journal on Black Women
Poets & Writers' 15th Birthday Book

Copyright © 1986 by Audre Lorde
All rights reserved.
Reissued as a Norton paperback 1994

Printed in the United States of America.

The text of this book is composed in Fairfield, with display type set in Elizabeth.
Composition and Manufacturing by Maple-Vail Book Manufacturing Group.
Book design by Antonina Krass

Library of Congress Cataloging-in-Publication Data
Lorde, Audre.
    Our dead behind us.
    I. Title.
PS3562.07508   1986   811´.54   85-29646

ISBN 0-393-31238-0

W. W. Norton & Company, Inc., 500 Fifth Avenue, New York, N.Y. 10110
W. W. Norton & Company Ltd., 10 Coptic Street, London WC1A 1PU
        7 8 9 0

to
Gloria I. Joseph

tikoro nnko agyina *

* Ashanti proverb: "one head cannot go into counsel"

Contents

Our Dead Behind Us

Sisters in Arms

The edge of our bed was a wide grid
where your fifteen-year-old daughter was hanging
gut-sprung on police wheels
a cablegram nailed to the wood
next to a map of the Western Reserve
I could not return with you to bury the body
reconstruct your nightly cardboards
against the seeping Transvaal cold
I could not plant the other limpet mine
against a wall at the railroad station
nor carry either of your souls back from the river
in a calabash upon my head
so I bought you a ticket to Durban
on my American Express
and we lay together
in the first light of a new season.

Now clearing roughage from my autumn garden
cow sorrel   overgrown rocket gone to seed
I reach for the taste of today
the *New York Times* finally mentions your country
a half-page story
of the first white south african killed in the "unrest"
Not of Black children massacred at Sebokeng
six-year-olds imprisoned for threatening the state
not of Thabo Sibeko, first grader, in his own blood
on his grandmother's parlor floor
Joyce, nine, trying to crawl to him
shitting through her navel
not of a three-week-old infant, nameless
lost under the burned beds of Tembisa

my hand comes down like a brown vise over the marigolds
reckless through despair
we were two Black women touching our flame
and we left our dead behind us
I hovered   you rose   the last ritual of healing
"It is spring," you whispered
"I sold the ticket for guns and sulfa
I leave for home tomorrow"
and wherever I touch you
I lick cold from my fingers
taste rage
like salt from the lips of a woman
who has killed too often to forget
and carries each death in her eyes
your mouth a parting orchid
"Someday you will come to *my* country
and we will fight side by side?"

Keys jingle in the door ajar   threatening
whatever is coming belongs here
I reach for your sweetness
but silence explodes like a pregnant belly
into my face
a vomit of nevers.

Mmanthatisi turns away from the cloth
her daughters-in-law are dyeing
the baby drools milk from her breast
she hands him half-asleep to his sister
dresses again for war
knowing the men will follow.
In the intricate Maseru twilights
quick   sad   vital
she maps the next day's battle

dreams of Durban   sometimes
visions the deep wry song of beach pebbles
running after the sea.

M-mán-tha-tisi: warrior queen and leader of the Tlokwa (Sotho) people during the mfe-
cane (crushing), one of the greatest crises in southern African history. The Sotho now
live in the Orange Free State, S.A.

Má-se-ru: scene of a great Tlokwa battle and now the capital of Lesotho.

Durban: Indian Ocean seaport and resort area in Natal Province, S.A.

To the Poet Who Happens to Be Black and the Black Poet Who Happens to Be a Woman

I

I was born in the gut of Blackness
from between my mother's particular thighs
her waters broke upon blue-flowered lineoleum
and turned to slush in the Harlem cold
10 PM on a full moon's night
my head crested round as a clock
"You were so dark," my mother said
"I thought you were a boy."

II

The first time I touched my sister   alive
I was sure   the earth took note
but we were not new
false skin peeled off like gloves of fire
yoked flame   I was
stripped to the tips of my fingers
her song written into my palms my nostrils my belly
welcome home
in a language   I was pleased to relearn.

III

No cold spirit ever strolled through my bones
on the corner of Amsterdam Avenue
no dog mistook me for a bench
nor a tree   nor a bone
no lover envisioned my plump brown arms
as wings   nor misnamed me condor
but I can recall without counting
eyes

cancelling me out
like an unpleasant appointment
postage due
stamped in yellow   red   purple
any color
except Black   and choice
and woman
alive.

IV
I cannot recall the words of my first poem
but I remember a promise
I made my pen
never to leave it
lying
in somebody else's blood.

Outlines

I
What hue lies in the slit of anger
ample and pure as night
what color the channel
blood comes through?

A Black woman and a white woman
charter our courses close
in a sea of calculated distance
warned away by reefs of hidden anger
histories rallied against us
the friendly face of cheap alliance.

Jonquils through the Mississippi snow
you entered my vision
with the force of hurled rock
defended by distance and a warning smile
fossil tears   pitched over the heart's wall
for protection
no other women
grown beyond safety
come back to tell us
whispering
past the turned shoulders
of our closest
we were not the first
Black woman white woman
altering course to fit our own journey.

In this treacherous sea
even the act of turning

is almost fatally difficult
coming around full face
into a driving storm
putting an end to running
before the wind.

On a helix of white
the letting of blood
the face of my love
and rage
coiled in my brown arms
an ache in the bone
we cannot alter history
by ignoring it
nor the contradictions
who we are.

II
A Black woman and a white woman
in the open fact of our loving
with not only our enemies' hands
raised against us
means a gradual sacrifice
of all that is simple
dreams
where you walk the mountain
still as a water-spirit
your arms lined with scalpels
and I hide the strength of my hungers
like a throwing knife in my hair.

Guilt wove through quarrels like barbed wire
fights in the half-forgotten schoolyard
gob of spit in a childhood street
yet both our mothers once scrubbed kitchens

in houses where comfortable women
died a separate silence
our mothers' nightmares
trapped into familiar hatred
the convenience of others drilled into their lives
like studding into a wall
they taught us to understand
only the strangeness of men.

To give   but not beyond what is wanted
to speak   as well as to bear
the weight of hearing
Fragments of the word wrong
clung to my lashes like ice
confusing my vision with a crazed brilliance
your face   distorted into grids
of magnified complaint
our first winter
we made a home outside of symbol
learned to drain the expansion tank together
to look beyond the agreed-upon disguises
not to cry each other's tears.

How many Februarys
shall I lime this acid soil
inch by inch
reclaimed through our gathered waste?
from the wild onion shoots of April
to mulch in the August sun
squash blossoms   a cement driveway
kale and tomatoes
muscles etch the difference
between I need and forever.

When we first met

I had never been
for a walk in the woods.

III
light catches two women on a trail
together   embattled by choice
carving an agenda with tempered lightning
and no certainties
we mark tomorrow
examining every cell of the past
for what is useful   stoked by furies
we were supposed to absorb by forty
still we grow   more precise with each usage
like falling stars or torches
we print code names upon the scars
over each other's resolutions
our weaknesses   no longer hateful.

When women make love
beyond the first exploration
we meet each other   knowing
in a landscape
the rest of our lives
attempts to understand.

IV
Leaf-dappled the windows lighten
after a battle that leaves our night in tatters
and we two glad to be alive   and tender
the outline of your ear pressed on my shoulder
keeps a broken dish from becoming always.

We rise to dogshit   dumped on our front porch
the brass windchimes from Sundance stolen
despair offerings of the 8 A.M. News

reminding us we are still at war
and not with each other
"give us 22 minutes and we will give you the world . . ."
and still we dare
to say we are committed
sometimes without relish.

Ten blocks down the street
a cross is burning
we are a Black woman and a white woman
with two Black children
you talk with our next-door neighbors
I register for a shotgun
we secure the tender perennials
against an early frost
reconstructing a future we fuel
from our living   different precisions

In the next room a canvas chair
whispers beneath your weight
a breath of you between laundered towels
the flinty places that do not give.

V
Your face upon my shoulder
a crescent of freckle over bone
what we share   illuminates what we do not
the rest is a burden of history
we challenge
bearing each bitter piece to the light
we hone ourselves upon each other's courage
loving
as we cross the mined bridge   fury
tuned like a Geiger counter

to the softest place.

One straight light hair on the washbasin's rim
difference
intimate as a borrowed scarf
the children arrogant as mirrors
our pillows' mingled scent
this grain of our particular days
keeps a fine sharp edge
to which I cling like a banner
in a choice of winds
seeking an emotional language
in which to abbreviate time.

I trace the curve of your jaw
with a lover's finger
knowing the hardest battle
is only the first
how to do what we need for our living
with honor and in love
we have chosen each other
and the edge of each other's battles
the war is the same
if we lose
someday women's blood will congeal
upon a dead planet
if we win
there is no telling.

Stations

Some women love
to wait
for life   for a ring
in the June light   for a touch
of the sun to heal them   for another
woman's voice   to make them whole
to untie their hands
put words in their mouths
form to their passages   sound
to their screams   for some other sleeper
to remember   their future   their past.

Some women wait for their right
train   in the wrong station
in the alleys of morning
for the noon to holler
the night come down.

Some women wait for love
to rise up
the child of their promise
to gather from earth
what they do not plant
to claim pain for labor
to become
the tip of an arrow   to aim
at the heart of now
but it never stays.

Some women wait for visions
that do not return

where they were not welcome
naked
for invitations to places
they always wanted
to visit
to be repeated.

Some women wait for themselves
around the next corner
and call the empty spot peace
but the opposite of living
is only not living
and the stars do not care.

Some women wait for something
to change   and nothing
does change
so they change
themselves.

Equal Opportunity

The american deputy assistant secretary of defense
for Equal Opportunity
and safety
is a home girl.
Blindness slashes our tapestry to shreds.

The moss-green military tailoring sets off her color
beautifully
she says "when I stand up to speak in uniform
you can believe everyone takes notice!"
Superimposed skull-like across her trim square shoulders
dioxin-smear
the stench of napalm upon growing cabbage
the chug and thud of Corsairs in the foreground
advance like a blush across her cheeks
up the unpaved road outside Grenville, Grenada

An M–16 bayonet gleams
slashing away the wooden latch
of a one-room slat house in Soubise
mopping up   weapons search   pockets of resistance
Imelda   young   Black   in a tattered headcloth
standing to one side on her left foot
takes notice
one wrist behind her hip the other
palm-up beneath her chin   watching
armed men in moss-green jumpsuits turn out her shack
watching   mashed-up nutmeg trees
the trampled cocoa pods
graceless broken stalks of almost ripe banana
her sister has been missing now ten days

Beside the shattered waterpipe downroad
Granny Lou's consolations
    If it was only kill
    they'd wanted to kill we
    many more would have died
    look at Lebanon
    so as wars go this was an easy one
    But for we here
    who never woke up before
    to see plane shitting fire into chimney
    it was a damn awful lot!

The baby's father buried without his legs
burned bones in piles along the road
"any Cubans around here, girl? any guns?"
singed tree-ferns curl and jerk in the mortar rhythms
strumming up from shore   uphill a tree explodes
showering the house with scraps of leaves
the sweetish smell of unseen rotting flesh.

For a while there was almost enough
water   enough rice   enough quinine
the child tugs at her waistband
but she does not move quickly
she has heard how nervous these green men are
with their grenades and sweaty helmets
who offer cigarettes and chocolate but no bread
free batteries and herpes but no doctors
no free buses to the St. Georges market
no reading lessons in the brilliant afternoons
bodies strewn along Telescope Beach
these soldiers say are foreigners
but she has seen the charred bits of familiar cloth
and knows what to say to any invader
with an M−16 rifle held ready

while searching her cooking shed
overturning the empty pots with his apologetic grin
Imelda steps forward
the child pressing against her knees
"no guns, man, no guns here. we glad you come. you carry
water?"

The american deputy assistant secretary of defense
for equal opportunity and safety
pauses in her speech   licks her dry lips
"as you can see the Department has
a very good record
of equal opportunity for our women"
swims toward safety
through a lake of her own blood.

Soho Cinema

The woman who lives at 830 Broadway
walks her infant at twilight
through the neighborhood streets
warehoused   fashionably ugly
200-dollar silk blouses where hammers once hung
between the cafés and loading docks
chemicals bloom like wild roses in the gutter
her child in the tattersall pram
with an anti-nuclear sticker
takes it all in as possible
in an urban parlor.

Does she promise her daughter a life
on this island   easier   safer
than the ones they rush home to peruse
26 stories up over a bay
that is dying
the complex
double-crostic of this moment's culture?

When the six o'clock news is over
does the child pat her mother's wet cheeks
does she cradle her daughter against her
and weep for what she has seen
beside the bed under which they are lying
deathstink in the mattress
her son bayonetted to the door in Santiago de Chile
a corolla of tsetse flies crusting her daughter's nose
army hippos fire into the mourners
across Bleecker Street
blood on her Escoffier knives

blood welling in her garbage disposal
her baby's blood obscuring the screen
their next decade in living color
wired from pole to pole
when the six o'clock news is over
does she weep for what she has seen?

Or does she will her orange rebozo
with the Soho magenta fringe
to a Vieques campesina
six children and no land left
after the mortars
and the Navy
sailing into the sunset.

Vigil

Seven holes in my heart where flames live
in the shape of a tree
upside down
bodies hang in the branches
Bernadine selling coconut candy
on the war-rutted road to St. Georges
my son's bullet-proof vest
dark children
dripping off the globe
like burned cheese.

Pale early girls spread themselves
handkerchiefs in the grass
near willow
a synchronized throb of air
swan's wings are beating
strong enough to break a man's leg
all the signs say
do not touch.

Large solid women
walk the parapets beside me
mythic   hunted
knowing
what we cannot remember
hungry   hungry
windfall
songs at midnight
prepare me for morning.

Berlin Is Hard on Colored Girls

Perhaps a strange woman
walks down from the corner
into my bedroom
wasps nest behind her ears
she is eating a half-ripe banana
with brown flecks in the shape of a lizard
kittiwakes in her hair
her armpits smell of celery
perhaps
she is speaking my tongue
in a different tempo
the rhythm of gray whales praying
dark as a granite bowl
perhaps
she is a stone.

I cross her borders at midnight
the guards confused by a dream
Mother Christopher's warm bread
an end to war   perhaps
she is selling a season's ticket to the Berlin Opera
printed on the lid of a dim box
slowing the growth of rambler roses
perhaps   ice-saints have warned us
the tender forgiveness of contrasts
metal   silken thighs   a beached boat
perhaps   she is masquerading
in the american flag
in the hair-bouncing step
of a jaunty flower-bandit
perhaps

A nightingale waits in the alley
next to the yellow phone booth
under my pillow
a banana skin is wilting.

This Urn Contains Earth from German Concentration Camps

Plotzensee Memorial, West Berlin, 1984

Dark gray
the stone wall hangs
self-conscious wreaths
the heavy breath of gaudy Berlin roses
"The Vice Chancellor Remembers
The Heroic Generals of the Resistance"
and before a well-trimmed hedge
unpolished granite
tall as my daughter and twice around
Neatness
wiping memories   payment
from the air.

Midsummer's Eve beside a lake
keen   the smell of quiet
children straggling homeward
rough precisions of earth
beneath my rump
in a hollow root of the dead elm
a rabbit kindles.

The picnic is over
reluctantly
I stand   pick up my blanket
and flip into the bowl of still-warm corn
a writhing waterbug
cracked open   her pale eggs oozing
quiet
from the smash.

Earth
not the unremarkable ash
of fussy thin-boned infants
and adolescent Jewish girls
liming the Ravensbruck potatoes
careful and monsterless
this urn makes nothing
easy to say.

Mawu

In this white room full of strangers
you are the first face of love   remembered
but I belong to myself in the rude places
in the glare of your angriest looks
your blood   running through my dreams
like red angry water
and whatever I kill
turns in the death grasp
into your last   most beautiful
silence.

Released
from the prism of dreaming
we make peace with the women
we shall never become
I measured your betrayals
in a hundred different faces
to claim you as my own
grown cool   and delicate   and grave
beyond revision

So long as your death is a leaving
it will never be my last.

Departure sounds bell through the corridor
I rise and take your hand
remembering   beyond denials
I have survived
the gifts   still puzzling me
as in the voice of my departing mother

antique and querulous
flashes of old toughness   shine through like stars
teaching me how to die   insisting
death is not a disease.

Fishing the White Water

Men claim the easiest spots
stand knee-deep in calm dark water
where the trout is proven.

I never intended to press beyond
the sharp lines set as boundary
named as the razor names
parting the skin
and seeing the shapes of our weaknesses
etched into afternoon
the sudden vegetarian hunger for meat
tears on the typewriter
tyrannies of the correct
we offer mercy   forgiveness
to ourselves and our lovers
to the failures we underline daily
insisting upon next Thursday
yet forgetting to mention each other's name
the mother of desires
wrote them under our skin.

I call the stone   sister   who remembers
somewhere my grandmother's hand
brushed   on her way to market
to the ships
you can choose   not to live
near the graves where your grandmothers sing
in wind through the corn.

There have been easier times
for loving   different richness

if it were only the stars
we had wanted
to conquer
I could turn from your dear face
into the prism light makes
along my line
we cast into rapids
alone   back to back
laboring the current.

In some distant summer
working our way farther from bone
we will lie in the river
silent as caribou
and the children will bring us food.

You carry the yellow tackle box
a fishnet over your shoulder
knapsacked
I balance the broken-down rods
our rhythms pass through the trees
staking a claim   in difficult places
we head for the source.

On the Edge

A blade in the bed of a child
will slice up nightmare
into simpler hungers.

But a knife is a dangerous gift
girl brave enough to be crazy
you may never read this poem again
so commit it   like sin
or a promise   to the place
where poetry arms your beauty
with a hundred knives
some mined in the hills above Whydah
for a good-looking Creek
on the run.

The rhythms of your long body
do not yet move in my blood
but the first full moon of this year
is a void of course moon
I dream   I am precious rock
touching   the edge of you
that needs
the moon's loving.

Naming the Stories

Otter and quaking aspen
the set of a full cleansing moon
castle walls crumble
in silence
visions trapped by the wild stone
lace up the sky   pale electric fire
no sound
but a soft expectation of birds
calling the night home.

Half asleep   bells
mark a butterfly's birth
over the rubble
I crawl into dawn
corn woman bird girl sister
calls from the edge of a desert
where it is still night
to tell me her story
survival.

Rock speaks   a rooster language
and the light is broken
clear.

Diaspora

Afraid is a country with no exit visas
a wire of ants walking the horizon
embroiders our passports at birth
Johannesburg Alabama
a dark girl flees the cattle prods
skin hanging from her shredded nails
escapes into my nightmare
half an hour before the Shatila dawn
wakes in the well of a borrowed Volkswagen
or a rickety midnight sleeper-out of White River Junction
Washington bound   again
gulps carbon monoxide in a false-bottomed truck
fording the Braceras Grande
or an up-country river
grenades held dry in a calabash
leaving.

The Horse Casts a Shoe

The horse casts a shoe
edged cobbles are speaking
the journey ends in a wood
metal remains.

On the path
light catches two women upon a trail
heat rises like mist from the skin
unsaddled
the sacred and different
stretches to muscled limit
two women tremble
the spotty light trembles
limbs of hemlock weaving a shelter
above us
I tremble your season
unshod against mine.

We enter a landscape
seize likeness   lie down together
a horseshoe's clatter still ringing
our bodies bridged across terror
our names
a crostic for touch.

Reins

Refuse the meat of a female animal
when you are bearing
or her spirit may turn against you
and your child   fall in the blood.

Do not cook fish with bulging eyes
nor step over running water
the spirits of streams are restless
and can pull your child   down and away.

Do not joke with your grandfather
if you wish many strong children
nor hunt rabbits   in the afternoon

From the eighth day
when the child is named
to keep your milk flowing
do not eat coconut
after the sun goes down.

Wood Has No Mouth

When a mask breaks in Benin
the dancer must fast
make offerings
as if a relative died.

The mask cannot speak
the dancer's tears
are the tears of a weeping spirit.

Brown grain   mute
as a lost detail
Thoth
goddess of wisdom
disguised
as a baboon.

A Meeting of Minds

In a dream
she is not allowed
dreaming
the agent of control is
a zoning bee
her lips are wired to explode
at the slightest conversation
she stands
in a crystal
all around
other women are chatting
the walls are written in honey
in the dream
she is not allowed
to kiss her own mother
the agent of control
is   a white pencil
that writes
alone.

The Art of Response

The first answer was incorrect
the second was
sorry   the third trimmed its toenails
on the Vatican steps
the fourth went mad
the fifth
nursed a grudge until it bore twins
that drank poisoned grape juice in Jonestown
the sixth   wrote a book about it
the seventh
argued a case before the Supreme Court
against taxation on Girl Scout Cookies
the eighth held a news conference
while four Black babies
and one other   picketed New York City
for a hospital bed to die in
the ninth and tenth swore
Revenge on the Opposition
and the eleventh dug their graves
next to Eternal Truth
the twelfth
processed funds from a Third World country
that provides doctors for Central Harlem
the thirteenth
refused
the fourteenth sold cocaine and shamrocks
near a toilet in the Big Apple circus
the fifteenth
changed the question.

From the Cave

Last night an old man warned me
to mend my clothes
we would journey before light
into a foreign tongue.
I rode down autumn
mounted on a syllabus
through stairwells hung in dog
and typewriter covers
the ocean is rising
father
I came on time
and the waters touched me.

A woman I love
draws me
a bath of old roses.

A Question of Climate

I learned to be honest
the way I learned to swim
dropped into the inevitable
my father's thumbs in my hairless armpits
about to give way
I am trying
to surface   carefully
remembering
the water's shadow-legged musk
cannons of salt   exploding
my nostrils' rage
and for years
my powerful breast stroke
was a declaration of war.

Out to the Hard Road

The road to Southampton is layered with days
in different directions
you   driving an ecru sedan
through potato dust velvet   asphalt
beyond Patchogue   Yaphank   Ronkonkoma
and one of us always gave in
at the Center Moriches turn
the road narrows down to a sudden thirst
and Sally twirls her famed lemons
one eye out for the boys in blue.

Part of our secret lay hidden
in Monday's pocket   for comfort
we always go back
to our graves.

I never told you how much it hurt   leaving
casting myself adrift like a wounded ship
not the sharp edge of alone   kills
but no seen ending to over
reluctance   lining my mouth
potato dust   on the last shortcut
out
to a new September morning.

Every Traveler Has
One Vermont Poem

Spikes of lavender aster under Route 91
hide a longing or confession
"I remember when air was invisible"
from Chamberlin Hill down to Lord's Creek
tree mosses point the way home.

Two nights of frost
and already the hills are turning
curved green against the astonished morning
sneeze-weed and ox-eye daisies
not caring   I am a stranger
making a living choice.

Tanned boys I do not know
on their first proud harvest
wave from their father's tractor
one smiles as we drive past
the other hollers
nigger
into cropped and fragrant air.

For Judith

Hanging out
means being
together
upon the earth
boulders
crape myrtle trees
fox and deer
at the watering hole
not quite together
but learning
each other's ways.

For Jose and Regina

Children of war
learn
to grow up alone
and   silently
hoping
no one will notice
somebody's life could depend on it.

Children of war
know
the worst times
come announced
by a disagreeable whine
mother's rage   always
relieved
by a definite reason.

Beverly's Poem

I don't need to be rich
just able
to know how it feels
to get bored
with anemones.

Big Apple Circus

"Most of us out here don't think about
New York at all except as a zoo"

Used to be
the circus was for rich kids
every week in summer
I went by subway to the Bronx Zoo
Thursday was free day
the mandrill
scowling menace over his shoulder
shoves his crimson rump
into a nightmare now
grim tigers prowl shelved rock
tired of weeping.

The circus is a promise
silver dresses made of music
well-trained grins in a gaudy trick
the elephants' painted feet
that will not stamp out fools
nor advance to battle
up the Battery   across Maiden Lane
storming the Staten Island Ferry
clowns dive into nets that sing
and answer back
even the rifles fire flowers
but no bread
there are circuses in Pretoria
Moscow   Eau Claire   Alabama
soon there may even be a circus on the moon.

Between the acts
in littered alleys

tourists look like mourners
come to change their clothes
The seductive music hints
no more funeral marches
and we cannot hear the guns
across the river.

Florida

Black people fishing the causeway
full-skirted   bare brown to the bellyband
atilt on the railing   near a concrete road
where a crawler-transporter will move
the space shuttle from hangar to gantry.

Renting a biplane to stalk the full moon in Aquarius
as she rose under Venus between propellers Country Western surf
feasting on frozen black beans Cubano from Grand Union
in the mangrove swamp   elbows of cypress   scrub oak

Moon   moon   moon on the syncopated road
rimey with bullfrogs   walking beaches   fragrant and raunchy
fire-damp sand between my toes.

Huge arrogant cockroaches   with white people's manners
and their palmetto bug cousins
aggressive ridged slowness
the obstinacy of living fossils.

Sweet ugly-fruit   avocados   tomatoes
and melon in the mango slot
hibiscus spread like a rainbow of lovers
arced stamens waving
but even the jacaranda only last a day.

Crescent moon walking my sheets at midnight
lonely in the palmetto thicket   counting
persistent Canaveral lizards launch themselves
through my air conditioner
chasing equally determined fleas.

In Gainesville the last time there was only one
sister present who said   "I'm gonna remember your name
and the next time you come there'll be
quite a few more of us, hear?"
and there certainly was   a warm pool
of dark women's faces
in the sea of listening.

The first thing I did when I got home
after kissing my honey
was to wash my hair with small flowers
and begin a five-day fast.

Home

We arrived at my mother's island
to find your mother's name in the stone
we did not need   to go to the graveyard
for affirmation
our own genealogies
the language of childhood wars.

Two old dark women
in the back of the Belmont lorry
bound for L'Esterre
blessed us   greeting
Eh Dou-Dou you look *too* familiar
to you   to me
it no longer mattered.

Burning the Water Hyacinth

We flame the river
to keep the boat paths open
your eyes eat my shadow
at the light line
touchless
completing   each other's need
to yearn
to settle into hunger
faceless
a waning moon.

Plucking desire
from my palms
like the firehairs of a cactus
I know this appetite
the greed of a poet
or an empty woman
trying to touch
what matters.

Political Relations

In a hotel in Tashkent
the Latvian delegate from Riga
was sucking his fishbones
as a Chukwu woman with hands as hot as mine
caressed my knee beneath the dinner table
her slanted eyes were dark as seal fur
we did not know each other's tongue.

"Someday we will talk through our children"
she said
"I spoke to your eyes this morning
you have such a beautiful face"
thin-lipped Moscow girls translated for us
smirking at each other.

And I had watched her in the Conference Hall
ox-solid   black electric hair
straight as a deer's rein   fire-disc eyes
sweeping over the faces
like a stretch of frozen tundra
we were two ends of one taut rope
stretched like a promise from her mouth
singing the friendship song
her people sang for greeting
> There are only fourteen thousand of us left
> it is a very sad thing   it is a very sad thing
> when any people   any people   dies

"Yes, I heard you this morning"
I said   reaching out from the place where we touched
poured her vodka   an offering
which she accepted like roses

leaning across our white Russian interpreters
to kiss me softly upon my lips.

Then she got up and left
with the Latvian delegate from Riga.

Learning to Write

Is the alphabet responsible
for the book
in which it is written
that makes me peevish and nasty
and wish I were dumb   again?

We practiced drawing our letters
digging into the top of the desk
and old Sister Eymard
rapped our knuckles
until they bled
she was the meanest of all
and we knew she was crazy
but none of the grownups
would listen to us
until she died in a madhouse.

I am a bleak heroism of words
that refuse
to be buried alive
with the liars.

On My Way Out I Passed Over You and the Verrazano Bridge

Leaving   leaving
the bridged water
beneath
the red sands of South Beach
silhouette houses sliding off the horizon
oh love,   if I become anger
feel me
holding you in my heart   circling
the concrete   particular
arcs of this journey
landscape of trials
not to be lost in choice   nor decision
in the nape of the bay
our house slips under these wings
shuttle between nightmare and the possible.

The broad water drew us, and the space
growing enough green to feed ourselves over two seasons
now sulfur fuels burn in New Jersey
and when I wash my hands at the garden hose
the earth runs off bright yellow
the bridge disappears
only a lowering sky
in transit.

So do we blow the longest suspension bridge in the world
up from the middle
or will it be bombs at the Hylan Toll Plaza
mortars over Grymes Hill
flak shrieking through the streets of Rosebank

the home of the Staten Island ku klux klan
while sky-roaches napalm the Park Hill Projects
we live on the edge
of manufacturing
tomorrow or the unthinkable
made common as plantain-weed
by our act of not thinking
of taking
only what is given.

    Wintry Poland survives
    the bastardized prose of the *New York Times*
    while Soweto is a quaint heat treatment
    in some exotic but safely capitalized city
    where the Hero Children's bones moulder unmarked
    and the blood of my sister in exile Winnie Mandela
    slows   and her steps slow
    in a banned and waterless living
    her youngest daughter is becoming a poet.

I am writing these words as a route map
an artifact for survival
a chronicle of buried treasure
a mourning
for this place we are about to be leaving
a rudder for my children   your children
our lovers   our hopes   braided
from the dull wharves of Tompkinsville
to Zimbabwe   Chad   Azania
oh Willie sweet little brother with the snap in your eyes

what walls are you covering now
with your visions of revolution
the precise needs of our mother earth
the cost of false bread
and have you learned to nourish your sisters at last
as well as to treasure them?

Past darkened windows of a Bay Street Women's Shelter
like ghosts through the streets of Marazan
the northeastern altars of El Salvador
move the belly-wise blonded children of starvation
the once-black now wasted old people
who built Pretoria
Philadelphia   Atlanta   San Francisco
and even ancient London—yes, I tell you
Italians owned Britain
and Hannibal blackened the earth from the Alps to the Adriatic
Roman blood sickles like the blood of an African people
so where is true history written
except in the poems?

I am inside the shadow dipped upon your horizon
scanning a borrowed *Newsweek* where american soldiers
train seven-year-old Chilean boys
to do their killing for them.

Picture small-boned dark women
gun-belts taut over dyed cloth
between the baby and a rifle
how many of these women

activated plastique near the oil refineries
outside Capetown
burned their houses behind them
left
the fine-painted ochre walls
the carved water gourds still drying
and the new yams not yet harvested
which one of these women
was driven out of Crossroads
perched on the corrugated walls of her uprooted life
strapped to a lorry
the cooking pot banging her ankles
which one
saw her two-year-old daughter's face
squashed like a melon
in the pre-dawn police raids upon Noxolo
which one   writes poems
lies with other women
in the blood's affirmation?

History is not kind to us
we restitch it with living
past memory   forward
into desire
into the panic   articulation
of want   without having
or even the promise of getting.

And I dream of our coming together
encircled   driven
not only by love
but by lust for a working tomorrow
the flights of this journey
mapless   uncertain
and necessary as water.

Out of the Wind

to Blanche

For the days when the coffee grounds refuse to settle
and the last toothpick rolls into a crack on the floor
and all the telephone messages are from enemies
or for other people only
and the good old days
lie
between pages of books
we have already written
for the acorn of fear in each April
will this be the year
earth refuses
to forgive us with a blush of green
for the weary assumptions
of next winter's chill
and for silent days inbetween
your face
mingled in tulips
after brief rain.

Holographs

One hundred and fifty million truth seekers
at the trough of the evening news
arteries bumping and writhing
against Pik Botha's belly
a keg of sound
and how does it feel
to bury this baby you nursed for a year
weighing less than when she was born?

60,000 Pondo women keening
on the mountain
the smell of an alley in Gugeleto
after the burned bodies are dragged through
pennywhistles and stickdrum beats
earth under the high—arched feet
of deadly exuberant children
stones in their kneepants pockets
running toward Johannesburg
some singing   some waving
some stepping to intricate patterns
their fathers knew   tomorrow
they will be dead.

How can I mourn these children
my mothers and fathers
their sacred generous laughter
the arms' bright marrow
willow shadows upon the stair
Young men do not dream of dying
they seek the taut sinew
pulled   the passions of use

a latch slid into place
in the cold flickering light
the only dependable warmth
is the burn of the blood.

There Are No Honest Poems
About Dead Women

What do we want from each other
after we have told our stories
do we want
to be healed   do we want
mossy quiet stealing over our scars
do we want
the powerful unfrightening sister
who will make the pain go away
mother's voice   in the hallway
you've done it right
the first time   darling
you will never need
to do it again.

Thunder grumbles on the horizon
I buy time with another story
a pale blister of air
cadences of dead flesh
obscure the vowels.

A Question of *Essence*

In Arlesheim
the solstice smelled like hair pomade
the moon
caught between warm and forever
I dream of Alice Walker
her tears on my shoulder
but I cannot see her face
dark women painted clay pale
dash in and out of laughter
clay in their eyes   in their ears
around their noses
their tongues bedded down in clay
some are building shelters
against the past
low huts of seductive pictures
other beautiful women
Is Your Hair Still Political?
tell me
when it starts to burn . . .

For the Record

in memory of Eleanor Bumpers

Call out the colored girls
and the ones who call themselves Black
and the ones who hate the word nigger
and the ones who are very pale

Who will count the big fleshy women
the grandmother weighing 22 stone
with the rusty braids
and a gap-toothed scowl
who wasn't afraid of Armageddon
the first shotgun blast tore her right arm off
the one with the butcher knife
the second blew out her heart
through the back of her chest
and I am going to keep writing it down
how they carried her body out of the house
dress torn   up around her waist
uncovered
past tenants and the neighborhood children
a mountain of Black Woman
and I am going to keep telling this
if it kills me
and it might in ways I am
learning

The next day Indira Gandhi
was shot down in her garden
and I wonder what these two 67-year-old
colored girls
are saying to each other now

planning their return
and they weren't even
sisters.

Ethiopia

for Tifa

Seven years without milk
means everyone dances for joy
on your birthday
but when you clap   your hands
break at the wrist
and even grandmother's ghee
cannot mend
the delicate embroideries
of bone.

Generation III

Give back the life I gave
you   pay me my money down
so there's no question
I did it for love   for anything
but desire
put a tarnished nickel in my dish
so the guard will know
when he comes
with a bleeding chicken
tied to his wrist
with a bitter promise
that we are not kin
uncommitted forever.

Pay me what you cannot afford
to relinquish in rush hour streets
impaled on the high heels of women
jiggling and sweet
and tough as witches in a vineyard
where even your sweat smells
like love.

In the playground
children's voices are singing
Rise Africa You Will Be Free
a grown woman
steps over my rigid legs
stretched across the threshold of a kitchen
where pink and blue cakes cool in the window
on alternate days
you cradle me

dab lard on my right cheek
where the key to our house
burned a scar
the shape of your new name
in the enemy's tongue.

Never to Dream of Spiders

Time evaporates between the lips of strangers
my days collapse into a hollow tube
soon implodes against now
like an iron wall
my eyes are blocked with rubble
smears of perspectives
blurring each horizon
in the breathless precision of silence
one malignant word.

Once the renegade flesh was gone
fall air lay against my face
sharp and blue as a needle
but the rain fell through October
and death lay   a condemnation
within my blood.

The smell of your neck in August
a fine gold wire bejeweling war
all the rest lies
illusive as a farmhouse
on the other side of a valley
vanishing in the afternoon.

Day three   day four   day ten
the seventh step
a veiled door leading to my golden anniversary
flameproofed free-paper shredded
in the teeth of a pillaging dog

never to dream of spiders
and when they turned the hoses upon me
a burst of light.

Beams

In the afternoon sun
that smelled of contradiction
quick birds announcing spring's intention
and autumn about to begin
I started to tell you
what Eudora never told me
how quickly it goes
the other fork   out of mind's eye
choice
becoming a stone wall
across possible
beams
outlined on the shapes of winter
the sunset colors of Southampton Beach
red-snapper runs at Salina Cruz
and we slept in the fishermen's nets
a pendulum swing
between the rippling fingers
of a belly dancer with brass rings
and a two-year-old's sleep smell
the inexorable dwindling
no body's choice
and for a few short summers
I too was delightful.

Whenever spring comes I wish to burn
to ride the flood like a zebra goaded
shaken with sun
to braid the hair of a girl long dead
or is it my daughter grown
and desire for what is gone

sealed into hunger   like an abandoned mine
nights when fear came down like a jones
and I lay   rigid with denials
the clarity of frost without
the pain of coldness
autumn's sharp precisions and yet
for the green to stay.

Dark women clad in flat and functional leather
finger their breastsummers   whispering
sisterly advice   one dreams of fish
lays her lips like spring across my chest
where I am scarred and naked
as a strip-mined hill in West Virginia
and hanging on my office wall
a snapshot of the last Dahomean Amazons
taken the year that I was born
three old Black women in draped cloths
holding hands.

A knout of revelation   a corm of song
and love   a net of possible
surrounding all acts of life
one woman harvesting   all I have ever been
lights up my sky like stars
or flecks of paint   storm-flung
the blast and seep of gone
remains
only the peace we make with it
shifts into seasons
lengthening past equinox
sun   wind   come round again
seizing us in her arms like a warrior lover
or blowing us into shapes

we have avoided for years
as we turn
we forget what is not possible.

A *jones:* a drug habit or addiction.

Breastsummer: a breastplate; also a wooden beam across an empty place.

Call

Holy ghost woman
stolen out of your name
Rainbow Serpent
whose faces have been forgotten
Mother   loosen my tongue or adorn me
with a lighter burden
Aido Hwedo is coming.

On worn kitchen stools and tables
we are piecing our weapons together
scraps of different histories
do not let us shatter
any altar
she who scrubs the capitol toilets, listening
is your sister's youngest daughter
gnarled Harriet's anointed
you have not been without honor
even the young guerrilla has chosen
yells as she fires into the thicket
Aido Hwedo is coming.

I have written your names on my cheekbone
dreamed your eyes   flesh my epiphany
most ancient goddesses   hear me
enter
I have not forgotten your worship
nor my sisters
nor the sons of my daughters
my children watch for your print
in their labors
and they say Aido Hwedo is coming.

I am a Black woman   turning
mouthing your name as a password
through seductions   self-slaughter
and I believe in the holy ghost
mother
in your flames beyond our vision
blown light through the fingers of women
enduring   warring
sometimes outside your name
we do not choose all our rituals
Thandi Modise   winged girl of Soweto
brought fire back home in the snout of a mortar
and passes the word from her prison cell   whispering
Aido Hwedo is coming.

Rainbow Serpent who must not go
unspoken
I have offered up the safety of separations
sung the spirals of power
and what fills the spaces
before power unfolds or flounders
in desirable nonessentials
I am a Black woman   stripped down
and praying
my whole life has been an altar
worth its ending
and I say Aido Hwedo is coming.

I may be a weed in the garden
of women I have loved
who are still
trapped in their season
but even they shriek
as they rip burning gold from their skins
Aido Hwedo is coming.

We are learning by heart
what has never been taught
you are my given   fire-tongued
Oya   Seboulisa   Mawu   Afrekete
and now we are mourning our sisters
lost to the false hush of sorrow
to hardness and hatchets and childbirth
and we are shouting
Rosa Parks and Fannie Lou Hamer
Assata Shakur and Yaa Asantewa
my mother and Winnie Mandela are singing
in my throat
the holy ghosts' linguist
one iron silence broken
Aido Hwedo is calling
calling
your daughters are named
and conceiving
Mother   loosen my tongue
or adorn me
with a lighter burden
Aido Hwedo is coming.

Aido Hwedo is coming.

Aido Hwedo is coming.

Aido Hwedo: The Rainbow Serpent; also a representation of all ancient divinities who
must be worshipped but whose names and faces have been lost in time.